When Doves Cry

Sinclair Azubuike Farrell

TaMaRe
HOUSE

When Doves Cry

The right of Sinclair Azubuike Farrell to be identified as Author of this work has been asserted in accordance with sections 77 and 78 of the Copyright, Designs and Patents Act, 1988.

First published in Great Britain with TamaRe House, April 2011

25 Brixton Station Road, London, SW9 8PB, United Kingdom
044 (0)844 357 2592, info@tamarehouse.com, www.tamarehouse.com

A CIP catalogue record for this book is available from the British Library.

This employs acid free paper and meets all ANSI standards for archival quality paper.

ISBN 9781906169-27-5

Printed and bound in Great Britain

Synopsis

'When Doves Cry' is a collection of beautifully written poems about everything from life, to modern society, love & so much more. A title chosen to reflect the deepest thoughts and sincerest emotions of a creative & emotionally expressive soul born and bred in London, England.

A wonderful book of poems comprised of both fascinating & inspirational poetry, written by the young Author & Poet Sinclair Azubuike Farrell. A book that once you read, you are never likely to forget!!!

Contents

Introduction

Hi, my name is Sinclair Azubuike Farrell. I am a Poet & Author. This is my second published poetry book, entitled 'When Doves Cry.'

It is a collection of over 40 of my poems written over a five year period. Writing poetry has proven to be a great way for me to express & share my deepest thoughts & feelings, creatively, with the world.

For my second book, I wanted to expand on my first book 'Paint a Perfect Picture', poetically by delving a lot deeper into my thoughts & imagination, to write poetry which displays a much greater reflection of the deepest areas of my mind.

I hope you enjoy this collection of my poems, as much as I enjoyed writing them. Thank you for reading.

Peace.

Acknowledgements

Thanks to my family, the Most High, my Ancestors and TamaRe House Publishers for helping to take my creative vision to greater heights.

Until The End of Time

Until The End of Time

Written 20th June 2010

Until the end of time
Words written
Engraved in the stone of history
Enshrined
On the mind
Of those who read
The letters combined
The signature of thoughts
Signed in each poetical line
Words echoed
To be remembered throughout time
When doves cry.

Haiti Earthquake: A World in Ruins

On 12th January 2010, The Caribbean country of Haiti was devastated by a massive 7.0-magnitude earthquake. The following poem is dedicated to those who died as a result of the devastation caused by the Earthquake, as well as those who lost loved ones as a result of the subsequent devastation.

Haiti Earthquake (A World in Ruins)

Written 17th January 2010

The Wind has blown
The leafs have scattered
& the birds have flown away

The clouds have thickened
The light has darkened
& bodies litter the crack filled shattered ground

Devastation is spread all around
Buildings have crumbled
In the blink of an eye
Homes and life's have been destroyed

A world in ruins
Desperately in need of healing
In remembrance of the memory
Of those who fell victim
To the disaster in Haiti.

New Beginning

New Beginning

Written 6th April 2005

Good times lately
May have been few
But today
Is the time to start a fresh
A time to start a new
Wash away past hurts
Prepare for tomorrow
Let go of yesterdays
Pain & sorrow
Life may not be all that exciting
Though embrace today
As it is the chance
For a new beginning.

Death of a Legend: Rest in Peace Michael Jackson

The next poem is one I wrote in tribute to a legend, a musical icon, someone who earned the title of 'The King of Pop' music. An artist who began his career as a child in the family group The Jackson 5. He then went on to achieve global fame as an adult solo artist with songs such as Billie Jean and Earth Song. His album Thriller, released in 1982, is the biggest-selling album of all time, selling 65m copies, according to the Guinness Book of World Records. Arguably the greatest entertainer of all time, his contributions and legacy will be felt upon the world forever. Rest in Peace Michael Jackson.

Death of a Legend: Rest in Peace Michael Jackson

Written 26th June 2009

A day of immense loss
For a whole family
Felt across the entire world

One of much pain and sorrow
For devoted devastated fans
Who lit candles
For what will be a sorely missed
Star and hero

A gentle creative soul
A troubled legend
But one deeply adored by millions
Loved for the music he created

Sneered at by critics
For the eccentric way he lived
Yet nobody could predict
That his life would end
As suddenly as it did

Thursday 25th June 2009
Saw the death of the most remarkable entertainer
Of all time

Whose popularity like no other
Transcended class, culture & colour lines

A superstar who performed
On the stage
Since the age of 5
Adored for his jaw dropping
Dance moves
And magnificent voice

An icon
Who left the world
With one amazing gift
Upon his unexpected tragic death
A wide array of much loved
Captivating music

An incredibly talented individual
Who will be fondly remembered
Upon the death of a legend
The world entered into a period
Of mourning

Rest in Peace
Michael Jackson
You will never be forgotten.

Fallen Heroes

Fallen Heroes

Written 26th February 2008

When your hero falls
It marks the end
Of an heroic yet tragic tale
Of a hero you not only admired
But found inspirational

Inspired by their attributes
And what they achieved in life
You stand by saddened
By their ultimate demise
And when the tragic day
Many saw coming
Actually arrives

Flowers & messages of sorrow
Are laid down in tribute
For a hero
Who has sadly died
Dedicated to all our Fallen Heroes
Of our time.

Star in the Sky

Star in the Sky

Written 8th April 2008

A star in the night's sky
Something to be gazed at
A fantastic sight
To be truly admired
The way it sparkles
So uniquely magical
In the reflective darkness of the night
Gazing at a star in the sky
Reflecting
To help make sense of life.

The Days of our Lives

The Days of our Lives

Written 14th June 2009

The days of our lives
Can resemble a dramatic
Soap opera at times
The ups and downs
The tears and laughter
Life can be like an unscripted drama
Each of us
As the uncredited actress or actor
In what is like a biographical film
Full of surprises
And a constant array of new characters
Each of us the star and the producer
Of the destiny of the film
Of our lives we star in
Directing the direction
In which, it heads in
With no script
Many scenes are often
Completely unexpected
An unpredictable tale
In which, we laugh and cry
During the joyous and emotional times
Lights, cameras, action
These are the days of our lives.

Swine Flu

Swine Flu

Written 19th July 2009

It's all over the news
The world is facing a global pandemic
Triggered by the outbreak of the virus
Known as the swine flu

But when I watch the news bulletins
On the TV or listen to the reports on the radio
Am I being told the truth?
Or am I and the rest of the public being lied to?

I want to know
WHO or what is truly responsible
For the creation of the H1N1 virus
The spread of which has created
Fear, confusion & concern amongst large numbers
Of the masses

Should I be concerned about the risk
Posed by the swine flu
And get myself vaccinated?
Or should I be more concerned about the logical truth
Presented in so called 'conspiracy theories'
Which are always dismissed?

Is the mainstream media circulating fear mongering
propaganda to create fear & chaos throughout the
population?
Is the real extent of this strain of flu, being sensationalized?
Or do I need to protect myself from the threat posed?

But what I really want to know
Blame it on my inquisitive mind
Is where did the swine flu actually come from?
& please don't tell me Mexico
Because I want to know the truth.

Through The Eyes of the Media

Through The Eyes of the Media

Written 22nd March 2009

A death played out on screen
A demise seen by all
Tuned in
A reality star, a daughter, a mother and a friend
To loved ones
By her side to the very end

We saw her live in the glitz and glamour
Of the celebrity lights
Her unexpected and surprising rise to dizzying heights
And on Mother's day 2009
The news circulated on radio and TV
That the 27 year old mother of two
Had finally died

In life she was often belittled and mocked
But in death she was mourned
Her gradual and slow death
Seen as tragic
By two faced hypocritical members of the public

Nonetheless
The death of an ordinary & simple woman
Who achieved fame & fortune
From out of almost nothing
I will remember
As unexpected star that died
In full view of us all
Through the eyes of the media.

Journey of Discovery

Journey of Discovery

Written 18th March 2009

My eyes have opened
My mind has awoken
The clearer my vision
The clearer the picture becomes
I can see things more clearly
And day by day
My memory
Is coming back to me

I'm starting to remember
Words, information & pictures
Are the trigger
Sparking that bright light of remembrance
Deep inside of me

It's going to be a long journey
But I know
It will be one of great discovery.

Starseed: Memory Loss

Starseed: Memory Loss

Written 17th March 2009

On a journey of discovery
Long since plunged
Into a state of amnesia
Slowly regaining my memory
Of who I am
And where I came from
I look to the stars
To find my home
In search of direction
I seek to be guided
Whilst lost and bewildered
Struggling to remember where home is
I look for clues and answers
In almost everything
I come across
If only remembered
What my purpose is
On this Earth
Then I could proceed to make a difference
I know I could.

To my Unborn Child

To my Unborn Child

Written 17th January 2009

To my unborn child
What sort of world
Can you expect when you are born?
I truly don't know
I hope
It is better than the one
I was born onto

Hopefully
I will be able to contribute
Towards help making it
A better world
For you

So that your future
Is not blighted
By pain and strife
I want you to live
The best possible life
In which, you will be blessed
With happiness and success

No doubt
You will be a chip off
The old block
And be wise, intelligent
And strong
Someone who doesn't follow the flock
A person who realises the benefits

Of being independent minded
Strong willed and confident

Never stray from the quest
To attain knowledge
Don't be afraid
To express your natural genius
You will be able to get by
Using your intelligence

I promise
From the day your mother
Gives birth
I will be there for you
Because you are my child
And even now I love you.

Welcome to a New World

Welcome to a New World

Written 28th November 2008

Welcome to a new world
Of hope, peace & prosperity
Where anything is possible
A world
Where men of each nation
Across the globe
Are united
Because of spiritual enlightment
Where all worshippers
Pray together
Instead of separately
In temples, mosques, synagogues
Or churches
A world where humanity
Is being led by right knowledge
Rather than being misled
By blissfully dangerous ignorance

A world where national armies and boarders
No longer exist
Where arms, nuclear weapons, famine
And death causing illnesses have vanished
Because of man's desire to live in peace
And scientist are no longer creating deadly
Diseases and viruses in laboratories
On the behalf of population controlling governments
And humans instead rely on plant based foods
As well as herbs
To cure ailments

Welcome to a new world
Which the brains and hands
Of men created.

Welcome to a new world
Which the brains and hands
Of men created.

999: The Final Frontier

999: The Final Frontier

Written 9th September 2009

The universally scripted end is near
Ascension of each cosmic traveller's soul
Commences as we approach the final frontier

Unparalleled Galactic activity increases
As the old world as we know it
As a whole
Shatters into fractured
Scattered pieces

The awakened soul
Stares upon the crumbling world
Thrusted into darkness
Torn from it clutches
Like a baby
From the arms of its weakened mother

The bewildered soul
Desperately seeks to cling on
Yet the world it used to know
Is no more

11:11 999
The countdown begins here
The door to a new path opens
As the soul approaches a captivating
Level of light
Eager at what it is bound to experience

It comes closer
To the final frontier
Of its Dimensional Evolution.

When Will Africa Be Free?

"For far too long, a majority of Africans have been indifferent to misrepresentations about who they are." - Childo Nwangwu

When Will Africa Be Free?

Written 4th February 2008

When will Africa be free?
Of political upheavals
Which, constantly hinder the economic
And social development of African people

Free to live in peace & harmony
Instead of in the midst
Of ongoing civil wars
Which threaten its nation's stability

When will Africa be free?
Of its vastly inflated debts
Imposed on it
By the west
Free to trade fairly
With European & Asian countries

When will the vast majority of Africans
Realise the significant spiritual, scientific and historic
contributions
They & their ancestors
Have given to the world?
Will it be before or after
They make every African country
A productive, safe, & prosperous haven
For African boys and girls?

When Will Africa be Free?

The day African people globally
Decide they want it to be.

African Holocaust

"It takes more than a horrifying transatlantic voyage chained in the filthy hold of a slave ship to erase someone's culture"- Maya Angelou

I wrote the poem 'African Holocaust' to somehow help with this cause. May we never ignore or forget the atrocities and injustices of the past.

African Holocaust

Written 23rd March 2008

A horrendous holocaust
So severe
The social, economical & psychological effects
Are still felt till this very day
A holocaust lasting for hundreds of years
A holocaust in which
Kidnapped people day and night
Lived in extreme states of fear

Towns & villages pillaged
Men kidnapped, enslaved and tortured
People stripped of their freedom
Sold to be forced into a life on enslavement
Females terrorised
By the never ending fear of being savagely
Raped or molested

A hellish experience
Of brutally enforced slave labour
Conducted by violent aggressors
Of various nationalities
Who wickedly treated adults and children
As three fifths of human beings

Free people kidnapped and enslaved
Against their will
Forced to survive in the depths of a real life nightmare
The Trans Atlantic sale and enforced labour
Of human life

Never seen before
A sad torturous, horrific holocaust.

Progression of His Race

I think the following two quotes by two men I admire greatly, say it all about the next poem….

"The future belongs to those who prepare for it today."- Malcolm X

"Up, you mighty race, accomplish what you will."- Marcus Garvey

Progression of His Race

Written 25th March 2005

A man
Who's articulate in the words
He speaks
Freedom he seeks
Prepared to lay his life on the line
Like a soldier
On the frontline
In a battle of the minds
He defeats others with his intelligence
At the same time
Possessing confidence
Which, many mistake for arrogance
But this natural born leader
Is just confident
By learning from life valuable lessons
He talks with passion
When discussing
The progression of his race.

Imagine

Imagine

Written 19th February 2007

Can you imagine
A world without guns?
A community without bloodshed
Where homes were fixed
And nations united
A world, where we all co-exist
Without war and poverty
Why is it so hard to imagine
A world like this?

Innocent Child

Innocent Child

Written 28th November 2008

In memory of Delayno and Romario Mullings- Sewell and Peter Connelly (Baby P)

Children can be so instinctively joyful, happy & playful
But adults can be horribly cruel
In ways that are truly unimaginable

A child's eyes can see so much
Yet some never get to see a glimmer of happiness
Or a touch of their mother's love

Beautiful baby boys and girls
Who should be cherished, loved and protected
By the parents by whom they were created
Are subjected to misery, pain and sickening violence
Instead of being adored for the natural childish innocence

In each story
Lays a complete and utter tragedy
A child's life of so much future potential and possibility
Is ended so cruelly

How any adult can be so wickedly cold
And so brutally violent
To a young innocent child
Many of us, fortunately will never know
But wherever your innocent souls are now
May they be in peace
Baby P, Delayno & Romario.

Child of the Universe

Child of the Universe

Written 25th November 2009

Child of the Universe
Travelling on a light bearing path
Through the vastness of the stars

A galactic soul
Incarnating onto Earth
To once again experience
The 3rd density physical reality

On a journey of growth
On a soul level
Charged with much energy
In tune with higher frequencies
Functioning with a greater vibration

Here to help contribute greatly with Earth's many changes
Aware of their implications Universally
Aligning closely with Earth's heartbeat
Dear Mother nature

Experiencing an intriguing period of conscious awakening
The result of a tremendous DNA explosion
Defined by the highest frequency of the number 9

As a child of the cosmos
Here on Earth
Only for a limited period of time.

Drifting with the Wind

Drifting with the Wind

Written 18th April 2009

In a mind of much contemplation and deep thought
I know I won't be around for long
A wounded heart
Dictates to me that it's better not to get attached to anyone

Drifting with the wind
Without a close friend
No soul apart from my own
On Which, I can depend
Alone in the cold
Forever on the outside looking in

Loneliness is a cold, miserable place
In which, your hearts hardens
Your tears becomes warm
Before your tear ducts close
To never again release the pain of your afflicted soul
Burdened heavily by the issues of the world

A cold abandoned lonely soul
Walks on the road of fate alone
Never getting attached to anyone
For too long
Before their heart compels them to move on
Once again
Like a leaf fallen from a tree
Forever drifting in the wind.

Egypt on My Mind

I wrote the next poem while in the country of Egypt; visiting for the first time on coincidently what was also my first time travelling out of my country of birth. My first time on a plane is something on its own that I will never forget and my 2 weeks in Egypt proved to be an absolutely unique, joyous & unforgettable experience. From quad biking in the desert, taking a boat trip across the red sea, to seeing the pyramids and sphinx of Giza, visiting Egypt was a fantastic experience.

Egypt on My Mind

Written 19th May 2009

Egypt is on my mind
The land of Gods & Goddesses
Of Ancient times

Isis & Osiris
The land once
Known as Kemet
Because of it's highly melaninated
Original inhabitants

Returning to the motherland
For an honoured treasured spiritual experience
Valued and treasured
From the minute
It begins
To the second it ends

Fate can take you many places
Very few as magical as this
A divine gift from those who watch over
Our planet

On the path of my destiny
I travel through different time zones
Like a free flying bird
Waking up in a completely
Different country

With Egypt on my mind

I follow my heart
& the journey home
Has just begun.

I follow my heart
& the journey home

Like A Bird

Like A Bird

Written 5th May 2009

Like a bird
Not confined by limiting restrictions
On its life
My mind acts as my wings
Which, I use to fly away
From the harsh reality
Which, surrounds me

On a boundless planet
With various species
I travel amongst them
In search of peace
From the cruel nightmares
Flooding the environment
I see

The vision which, I fly to
Are not of the past or present
But of the yet determined future
In which, I desire to live
I travel past the blue cloudy sky
Of the day
To arrive in the star filled
Dark night sky
As the hectic world
Fastly passes me by

I don't know where home is
So I ponder and reflect
On what I've seen
Where I go
Wondering when the sun rises
On a dawn of a new day
Across the planet
Where will I be?
Will I find myself locked in seclusion to be alone?
Or will I find other birds like me?

I often look up at the sky
Like an adventurous care free bird
I aim high
So that I can fly
To where I want to be.

Angels without Wings

Angels without Wings

Written 2nd June 2009

An appearance cloaked in disguise
Angels without wings
Guardians of the light
Those who chose to descend
From beyond the sky
Born to take flight
To show the world
A new way of life
With an intentional purpose on earth
The souls who will plant the seeds
For the growth and evolution
Of the collective consciousness of humanity
The torch bearers of a loving change
Souls of the stars
Seeds from unimaginable depths of the galaxy
The ones here to help maintain
The planets destiny
On earth as we speak
Unrecognisable, angels without wings.

Human & the Beast

Human & the Beast

Written 19th February 2007

If you put an animal
Into a jungle
And traumatise it
When it's young
It will become a wild beast
When it's older
If it indeed lives that long.

Gangland Britain

Gangland Britain

Written 25th January 2009

Gangland Britain
A criminal social structure
Of organised crime bosses
Down to crazed young thugs

An almost lawless state
Ruled by fear, intimidation
And violence
In which victims
Are often kept permanently silent
Fearless hooded yobs
Run riot
Terrorising entire neighbourhoods
Through violence
And anti social methods

Police struggling to maintain
Law and order
Rising crime levels
And plenty of violent murders
Often the consequences
Of long standing feuds
Or petty disputes

Young males regularly
Shot or stabbed
Illegal arms
Smuggled into the country
By organised criminal gangs

Capitalising on the murder rate
And the thirst for firearms

Welcome to Gangland Britain
A minefield of senseless stabbings, shootings
Street crime, armed robberies and gangland executions

A dangerous place for most
Where crime has almost
Spiralled out of control
Like a social disease
Affecting the streets
Of crime ridden
Gangland Britain.

War on Terrorism

War on Terrorism

Written 10th April 2005

Good evening ladies and gentleman
How are you doing on this fine evening?
I'm the Nubian poet
A poetical ambassador of the City
Where you find the House of Commons

I've come to read you
A deep poem
Written weeks before England's 2005
General elections
Whilst discussing the bogus war on terrorism

Which, has been fabricated
To crush the remaining vestiges of democracy and
nationalism
In the west
Do your best
To stay with me

Triggered by anticipated events on September 11th
Think back to the collapsing of the twin towers
Which, was supposedly masterminded
By, the CIA trained Osama Bin Laden
Who coincidently with all the sophiscated intelligence
In the world
Is still missing
He must be sitting comfortably within those mountains

This climate of fear

Created by the threat
Of Muslim terrorist attacks
Is an excuse to lay the foundations
For a police state
Where martial law could be declared
And those accused of being terrorist
E.g. those not being conned by the lie
Promoting the truth
Could be put under house arrest

While Muslims are the ones you hate
Think about the phoney 45 minutes
Weapons of mass destruction threat
Held by Saddam Hussein
Blair & Bush, so called Christians
Never managed to find where they were hidden

Join the dots and find the connection
To see how a global plague could be released
In coming years to kill billions
Deny it as pure speculation
I won't be part of the public denial mechanism

Do you hear the roar
Of the beast?
As a debit/credit card, cashless society nears
Is the mark of the beast already here?

As a New world order
Dawns even closer
As those in power
Declare a war on terror

It's not all about Al Qaeda

When it comes to the war on terrorism
I urge you to search out the truth
And I leave it at that
Good night ladies and gentlemen.

Riot to end All Riots

Riot to end All Riots

Written 14th December 2008

It's been predicted
That there will be a riot
A deadly ferocious riot
Of fire looting & widespread violence
Public disorder and chaos

A fierce battle
Between riot police
And thousands upon thousands
Of disgruntled members of the public

A riot on a level
Which, has never been seen before
Where the state to curb the social upheaval
Will declare martial law

Armed soldiers will patrol the streets
And curfews will be implemented
In a bid to end social disorder
Plenty will be arrested
And hospitals will be full
Of blood soaked injured disorientated patients
A result of petrol bombs being thrown
Blunt objects being used
Or guns being fired

In a riot
Which, the police won't be heavy handed just plain dangerous

A riot so serious
Even some of the most dedicated anarchist
Will be frightened
Not prepared for what is to happen
In a riot
On such a scale
Which, has never been seen
All other riots will look peaceful in comparison

Transport links will be cancelled
Shops will be shut down
Roads will be closed
And for those who want no part of it
Will be warned to stay at home
Lock their doors and make sure all windows are shut
Because no one will be sure to be safe
When this riot begins.

Running

Running

Written 31st May 2005

Running as fast as I can
Not in a competition
To win first prize
But as the hunted prey
Running through the bushes
Sweating nervously
Breathing heavily
Trying to escape
Desperately
Trying to figure out
The right way to turn
They're getting closer
If they catch me
I'll burn
I can hear the blood thirsty dogs
Barking
As if they're right behind me
Hot on my heels
Running to be free
Or face the rest of my life in captivity
As another mindless slave
For a capitalistic system
I'll be running for my freedom
To the day I'm dead and buried.

The Coming Ice Age

The Coming Ice Age

Written 17th January 2009

An age
Where man reverts
To living in caves
In order for him to escape
The extreme weather conditions
And his pending fate

A case of history repeating itself
Only affecting specific parts of the world
If only man listened
To the repeated warnings
He had been given

The polar ice caps melted
Sea levels rose
Followed by widespread flooding

It's happened before
It will happen again

What will we do?
If only man knew
The exact carnage
The weather would reap
On the world
Then maybe man would prepare
For the worse
The impact of what climate change
Will have on the world.

Time Will Tell

Time Will Tell

Written 25th February 2009

Dedicated to Cd

Only time will tell
What the years ahead
Have in store
Will they be full of completely unexpected surprises
Which shock the world?
Bringing about a dramatic change in life
For us all
Time itself holds the secrets
Which, are yet to be revealed
In due course
They slowly but surely will
That is the promise that time holds
Forever waiting in the shadows
To reveal the truth
Time has something
To reveal to us all.

Rivers of Blood (2008)

Rivers of Blood (2008)

Written 18th March 2008

Passions run high
When discussing the subject
Of nationhood and race
People remained divided
By not only a lack of understanding
But by feelings of hate.

A large multi-cultural society
Separated by the undeniable
Colour lines
Of different communities

Racial tension, stereotypes
Institutionalized covert and overt racism
Still persist
While these communities of racial and religious groups
Co-exist

Maybe it's been said before
But when the colour man's skin
Is no longer an issue
Only then will we not be close
To a riotous race war.

The 144, 000

The 144, 000

Written 24th February 2009

Many will be called
Few will be chosen
Some would have awoken
And realised what's coming

Souls will rise
To the highest level of consciousness
Light bearers
Born onto the planet
To help awaken the unconscious masses

Born to live in accordance with nature
And in the image
Of the most high creators

Earth will witness many changes
144,000 here to aid the humanity and the planet
Through reality shattering experiences.

Lambs to the Slaughter

Lambs to the Slaughter

Written 25th November 2008

Mindless idle followers
Absolutely clueless
To where they are ultimately
Being led

Eyes wide shut
Led blindly
To an horrific fate
Which, awaits thee

The wicked deceitful shepherd
Guides the hapless flock
Foolishly eager with anticipation
Of what awaits them
At the end of the path
On which, they walk
Without a questioning thought

Idle followers
Walking eagerly behind one another
Yet each one
Is another
Naive innocent lamb
Being led to the slaughter.

The Truth about the Recession

The Truth about the Recession

Written 8th January 2009

If you are easily offended
Then you probably won't like
The following statement
The best thing about the recession
Is it allows money hungry corporate employers
To excusably cut costs
Helping to increase profit made
By making thousands of employees fearing for their jobs,
redundant

The credit crunch and the recession
Are a controlled set of events
A cruel horrible sort of game
Being thrusted on the unwitting public
By those with political power
And experts of finance

If only most of us realised
Then maybe, just maybe
We could do something about it
Ask further in depth questions
Of politicians, those working in the financial centre
Of the world
The city of London
As well as those who own the federal-reserve
And the bank of England

What are the real reasons
For the credit crunch?
Why did high street banks issue mortgages
To individuals
Whose credit history clearly indicated
That they would be unable to afford repayments?
Why would they do this?
Was it to further their- own interests?

The actions and attitudes
Of the government and the bank
In the pre-instigated financial crisis
Are quite literally scandalous
Especially as the governments
Include tax payer's money
In financial packages
To bail out banks
Whilst hundreds upon hundreds
Of members of the public's homes
Are repossessed each month

Politicians lie to our faces
Likely laughing behind our backs
Put spin on the truth
Constantly use rehashed rhetoric
And distort the facts
Fooling some of the public
Some of the time
Going to great lengths to deceive the majority
All year round

The government of England
Doesn't even have control
Of its national currency

The pound
Those individuals who do and own the Bank of England
Have purposely driven its value down

Surely the public has to be aware
Now that the recession
Didn't happen by accident
A process created on purpose
By unscrupulous heads of banks
Our elected political leaders
And other powerful members
Of a global elite

I apologise again
If you were offended by anything
I've said
I just thought you might want to know
About the truth about the recession.

2 Wings of a Bird

2 Wings of a Bird

Written 14th January 2009

The left and right wing
Are two wings
Of the same bird
There is practically no difference
The closer you look
The more similarities
You will see

If you were to examine them both
You would discover
They are like two leafs
Off the same tree
And like two separate
Western political parties
You would notice
There is very little difference
To the left wing or right wing
Contrary to popular belief.

World at Risk

World at Risk

Written 4th December 2008

Sky news
Will warn us about terrorist
Hell bent on attacking us
Because they supposedly
Envy the western way of life
And resent Britain & America's foreign policy

But Sky, ITN, BBC or any other news channel on TV
Won't inform us about high ranking individuals
Apart of secret societies
Controlling the world
Through law, economics and politics

The ones powerful enough to use the media
To spread propaganda
To further their agenda
Of total political, economical, social and environmental
Control of the world
And the vast majority of its people

These Masonic doomsday occultists
Have trained angered and used terrorist
To create attacks
Which, allows them to legally introduce
Uncontested draconian legislations
Under the banner of protecting the public
From the threat of terrorism

But whether you believe me or not

It's time the world wake up
To what's going on around us
Before it's too late
Because these satanic masons
Will not hesitate in launching
A deadly weapon of mass destruction attack
To destroy the United States or any other western target
By 2013
To increase their power
In order to introduce to the world
A fascist new one world order

A subject mentioned in numerous books
On various websites and by many public speakers
But practically never
In the mainstream media
Which, prefers to give us the impression
That the western world is under siege by Islamic terrorist

And it won't tell us
About the billionaire plus bankers & industrialists
As well as presidents, prime ministers, politicians and high
ranking religious leaders amongst others
Apart of satanic orders of secret societies
Are truly the ones
Willing to put the world at risk.

Rainbow Warriors

Rainbow Warriors

Written 22nd June 2009

Rainbow Warriors
Warriors of the spirit & light
Light of love & truth
Now is our time
To help liberate mother earth

As it has been predicted
A powerful spirit
Is now sweeping across the planet
Bringing forth global changes
As we move forth
Into the age of Aquarius

In the Native American Vision
The term rainbow expresses
That this is to be a global event
Not limited
To tribe, nation or race

We are here for the same purpose
Yet we travel from separate depths of the universe
Stationed on specific locations on earth
We must stand up now
To help protect humanity
And help the planet evolve

Rainbow warriors
We must rise up our swords
Of light

Because now is our time
To change the world.

Hearts to Africa

Hearts to Africa

Written 12th January 2008

We her children have travelled far and wide
But our hearts belong to our mother
The world knows her as Africa

When she suffers
We naturally want to ease her suffering
Because we love her

As her children
It's our natural reaction
To try and make things better

She has provided so much for us
To help us grow, live and survive
Yet at times
We have been so helpless
To stop those who wanted to take advantage
Of what she has to offer

She is blessed with elements of nature
And although circumstances
Mean we have been separated

Maybe one day
Her children who have lost their way
Will return home
And we will be together.

Stolen Legacy

Stolen Legacy

Written 12th April 2008

You can rob an uneducated fool
Of his history
But you can't take away
A wise man's memory

You can lie about what took place
In the past
But for how long
Will the period of the truth
Being kept from coming out, last?

How long are stolen artefacts
Going to be kept in foreign museums?
To be conveniently kept out of sight
Out of mind

How many more books
Are racially biased authors
Going to write?
Based on distortion of the truth
And outright lies

Because you can distort the facts
And put forward a falsified history
But when you rob a man of his spiritual
Or cultural heritage
As well as his historical identity
And claim it as your own
It will always be a stolen legacy.

African Cultural Schools important for our Survival

African Cultural Schools important for our Survival

Written 16th January 2008

In the 21st century and beyond
African cultural schools
Are extremely vital
For our survival
As a forward thinking progressive group of people

What would be taught?
And who would teach it?
Is up to us
How long are we going to accept
The children of our community, the future of families
Being provided with a sub standard free education
Do we not want to awaken their natural genius?

Allow them to excel in the sciences
In all areas of biology, chemistry and physics
Allow them to learn about the importance of our environment
What foods help to maintain a healthy, nutritious diet
Promoting natural medicines
And their ability to heal

How do you feel?
About your children being taught a multitude
Of global and cultural languages
The likes of Swahili, mandarin & English

Schools which provide them with a high level of
understanding of mathematics

African children just like any other
Need to have a clear understanding
Of the world story
The relationship between Africans, Asians, Europeans and
others, past and present
How Africans built prosperous empires
Civilizations and many modern inventions
Throughout the ages
Highlighting the countless achievements
Yet not ignoring the many setbacks, tragedies and failures

Educating the mind is a never ending process
By far the most life changing
Any human will experience

We must equip our future generations
With the skills of how to function
Productively and successfully
In life, together with the rest of the world
Instilling in them nation building skills

Doing this while providing children
With an understanding of African cultures
Before they enter into adulthood
After going through their rights of passage

Also nurturing the children spiritually
Teaching them about the truthful origins
Of the major world religions
The numerous spiritual concepts
Of our ancient ancestors

As well as the spiritual importance
Of ancestral spirits
In many African cultures

All these elements and more of teaching
In African cultural schools
Is imperative
Because a quality well rounded education
Helps to build strong affluent nations

How long are any group going to depend on others
Who have not got their best interests at heart
To educate their children?

Oh Almighty Sirius

Sirius, honoured by many ancient cultures, is the brightest star in the night sky on reflecting on its beauty and uniqueness as an admirer of the night time sky, I wrote the following poem about it.

Oh Almighty Sirius

Written 29th October 2009

Sirius
Oh almighty Sirius
The brightest star
Glowing in the sky
From much distance
A beacon of magnificence
You shine down upon Earth
With unparalleled excellence

Sirius
Oh almighty Sirius
A torch of light
You shine magnificently
In the depths
Of unimaginable darkness

Sirius
Oh almighty Sirius.

Galactic Federation of Light
Message from the Cosmos

Galactic Federation of Light Message from the Cosmos

Written 11th January 2009

Man must lay down the arms
Stop the war
Open themselves up to the Universe
The messages
All around us

As we pass swiftly
Into the Age of Aquarius
A time of peace and evolution
For worthy accepting humans
We are all free
To accept or reject
The consequences of Earths changes

For those who learn to live in peace
Will pass onto the higher realms
Of spiritual evolution

Be warned though
There are many evil false prophets and guides
Who will take from you
Whilst on this Earth
In exchange for worthless rubbish
In return

Learn to take heed
Of the voice within

That which, can help decipher
What is truth, what is chaos, untruth
And simply confusion

The voice of truth within
Will help lead you onto the path
Of evolution
Gradually you will learn
To live without fear
To seek the truth
Seek to know yourself
Why you exist
And to live in harmony with planet Earth

Now look inside your soul
And realise
You have been blessed by the supreme
Love and truth of the cosmos.

A Brand New World Order

A Brand New World Order

Written 6th January 2009

Regardless of what you may have heard
Don't be deterred
From envisaging a better world

A new world
Is on the horizon
To be created in the minds
Of visionary's, first
A world where peace and prosperity
Sweep across the entire Earth

Tyranny in any land
Will cease to reign
Instead, shall be replaced
By fair and equal social justice
For all men

Wars will be no more
And no longer
Will Earth be burdened
By destructive conflicts
Being fought

As a result of humanity
Realigning itself spiritually
With the guiding forces
Of our vast universe

Religion's stranglehold

Over man's spiritual side
Would have ended
No longer capable of being used as a tool
To conquer, deceive and control the masses

In a new world order
The world's wealth
Will be equally divided
Its abundance of natural resources
Will not be exploited or wasted
But instead will be fairly utilised
For the entire planet's benefit

The world will see great change
Never to be the same again
A new world order in place
One of love, peace, harmony & justice
A brand new world order
Across the entire planet.

Return to the Hood

Return to the Hood

Written 11th January 2009

We've come a long way
From where we first started
Forgetting where we came from
Ignoring our roots

We used to live in natural environments
Surrounded by fresh air
And Clean water

Now we dwell in filthy stinking dumping grounds
We call council estates, garrisons, housing projects
Ghetto's or shanty towns
Where we argue with neighbours
Because of loud music
Or some other pettiness

How we've allowed ourselves
To decline to such a state
Would leave those
Who came before us
Amazed

We used to value ourselves
Now we just want to look
And act like anybody else
But ourselves

It's sad, pitiful and shameful
How bad things have got

We were like Gods in the flesh once
Now we're a shadow
Of our former self's

It's got to that stage
Many of us know we should
But how many of us will
Return to a state of God hood.

When Doves Cry

When Doves Cry

Written 31st January 2009

The cries of Doves
Can't be heard
Yet they do
In the silence of the night
When no one can hear their silent cries

Doves cry
Because they are hurting
In severe pain
In need of healing

Their wounds & scars
Can be seen from afar
But they are ignored
Because it seems no one cares

What troubles their heart's
Is the burdens & pains of life
From which, they can't escape

Even if they could fly beyond the clouds & sky
To the heavens of tranquillity
These hurt doves will continue
To cry in pain
Until they are healed properly

If only the world could hear
The sound of
When doves cry.

Recommended Books

The following is a list of books I highly recommend.

Spot the Difference: Raising your game to reach your full potential
By Swiss- So Solid (Published by Tamare House)

Legacy of the Black Gods - In Time before time (Coming forth from The Akashic Records)
By Paul Simons (Published by Tamare House)

Return of the Elohim - (Behold the Rise of the Cosmosans 999)
By Paul Simons (Published by Tamare House)

The African Origin of Civilization: *Myth or Reality*
By Cheikh Anta Diop

Great Black Heroes: *Five Notable Inventors*
By Wade Hudson

Melanin: *A Key to Freedom*
By Richard King M.D

Vitamins and Minerals: *From A to Z*
By Jewell Pookrum

The Black Holocaust: *For Beginners*
By S.E Anderson

African Names: *Reclaim Your Heritage*
By Samaki (Sharon J Bernhardt)

The Secret
By Rhonda Byrne

Rich Minds, Rich Rewards
By Valorie Burton

Secrets of the Millionaire Mind: *Think Rich to Get Rich*
By T. Harv Eker

The Science of Getting Rich: *Attracting Financial Success through Creative Thought*
By Wallace D. Wattles

The Rose That Grew From Concrete
By Tupac A Shakur

Paint a Perfect Picture

By Sinclair A Farrell
(ISBN: 978-1-906169-22-0)
(Published by TamaRe House)

www.tamarehouse.com/paintaperfectpicture

Author Details

To contact Author Sinclair A. Farrell, use the Poetical TV details below.

Poetical TV was first established online in April 2009, by British born Poet & Author Sinclair Azubuike Farrell. It was created with the objective of sharing the creative gift of Poetry with a worldwide audience, whilst seeking to entertain, inform & inspire others through various creative concepts.

Email Poetical TV @ **poeticaltv@live.co.uk**

Poetical TV Website: **www.poeticaltv.webs.com** (Subject to Change)

Follow Poetical TV on Twitter @ **www.twitter.com/poeticaltv**

Visit Poetical TV YouTube Channels-
www.youtube.com/poeticaltv or
www.youtube.com/poeticaltvlive

Bonus Poem

The Next Chapter

Written 12th January 2011

Turn the page

The end has come

The day before is over

Forever we say goodbye to the old past

Before we can embrace a new future

Distant memories will shortly fade away

As we wake up to face a new day

Starting all over again

A fresh start, on a new page

Neither is it the end or the beginning

As we turn the pages

To the next chapter.

By Sinclair Azubuike Farrell.

PEACE!!!!

CPSIA information can be obtained at www.ICGtesting.com
Printed in the USA
LVOW12s1516071213

364283LV00003B/270/P